THE
DO IT YOURSELF
DEGREE

Jay Cross

How To Earn Your Bachelor's Degree in 1 Year Or Less, For Under $10,000

Without Classes, Homework, or Student Loans

"Formal education will make you a living. Self-education will make you a fortune."

- Jim Rohn

DIY Degree Table of Contents

Foreword

In 1995, *Change Magazine* published a classic article by Barr and Tagg titled "From Teaching to Learning", which starts out by saying "A paradigm shift is taking place in American higher education. In its briefest form, the paradigm that has governed our colleges is this: A college is an institution that exists to provide instruction. Subtly but profoundly we are shifting to a new paradigm: A college is an institution that exists to produce learning. This shift changes everything..."

The authors relate later in the article that this insight had actually been noted in another article some 20 years earlier. So here we are 40+ years later, and the debate still rages: what are colleges and universities really for?

To teach? To produce learning? To enable students to obtain the credentials that employers are looking for?

There have been some indications of progress—the introduction of technologies which facilitate learning has been impressive, for example, although at times it appears random and even misguided. But institutions of higher education are basically still as they have been
since the late 19th century: about acquiring and demonstrating knowledge according to a well-defined standard.

That's a good start, and it's not enough. Literacy today is no longer just about reading and writing; being literate is about demonstrating the knowledge, skills and attitudes that allow one to survive and thrive in our rapidly changing world. A college degree is a credential that says you have earned the right to claim you have the knowledge. Your opportunity here is to go beyond that and demonstrate to your current or potential employers that you also recognize that they want more.

By using the techniques Jay outlines in this book, you will not only save yourself time and money in obtaining the credential, a degree, but you will also demonstrate that you are a person of action as well of knowledge, and that your attitude is one of being willing to jump in, design, plan, and take responsibility for executing a workable solution to expedite getting your degree. That can put you well ahead of the average college graduate in the escalating race to demonstrate real business value.

There is an even more subtle benefit. Because we have been schooled in the instruction paradigm for so long, often our default mental attitude is that if I am ignorant on some important subject, I need to go back to school and get another degree, or at least take the requisite courses to learn it. Upon completing the DIY Degree program, with a little reflection you will come to realize that you are a natural learner, you are learning all the time, much of it informally, but even when you intentionally set out to learn, you have many more options.

You can explore on your own what's needed, who or where are the best resources to engage for the approach to learning that works best for you, and how to design and execute a plan to get where you want to go.

You can even eventually reach the stage where, like many of us, you not only continue to acquire the knowledge, skills and attitudes that keep you performing at your desired level, but you can also experience the joy of learning and satisfaction of feeding your curiosity that come with such performance.

Good luck and Godspeed.

Professor Paul M Bauer
Clinical Professor Emeritus (and Inaugural Chairperson)
Department of Business Information & Analytics
Daniels College of Business
University of Denver

Chapter 1: My Own Story

My first day at my new school was rapidly becoming a disaster.

It was May, and I had just transferred to the University of Connecticut after getting my associates degree from Housatonic Community College in nearby Bridgeport, CT. About five minutes in, it dawned on me how night-and-day different the two schools were.

Housatonic (despite being a tiny school) was outstanding in almost every way. Their professors were sincere and dedicated. Their administrative staff was friendly and personable. Everyone wanted you to succeed and bent over backwards to help. It was, to my mind, everything a college should be.

UConn was the exact opposite. My first trip there was for an "advising session", which I assumed meant a one-on-one meeting with an academic advisor. Instead, I found myself sitting at a table with a dozen other transfer students for a scripted speech on how to pick your classes. The speech lasted about ten minutes, at which point we were given an arcane course completion sheet (see below), a phone book-sized course catalog, and a half-hearted "good luck" before the advisor scurried off.

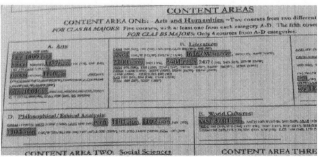

Looks almost like a court subpoena, doesn't it?

I was shocked.

Not to be denied, I marched into the advisor's office and asked for more direction. "I was hoping to leave here today with a full course schedule", I explained. Eventually, once every appeal to the course catalog failed to scare me off, she begrudgingly helped me pick out four courses that fit my degree program. (Which, excluding her stalling, took all of 15 minutes.) Everything about her demeanor screamed "don't get used to this."

She was right.

That day was a microcosm for how my entire (mercifully brief) time at UConn would go. During my one semester there, I encountered more apathy, frustration and foolishness than I can possibly describe. Policies that made no sense (and that no one explained.) Bursars who pretended that paying them was a privilege. Advisors who treated students like disruptions instead of customers. **And worst of all, course offerings that guaranteed you would be there for 100 years.**

As a transfer student, I needed roughly 12 more classes to finish my bachelor's. "I'll be done in no time", I thought. After all, I'd been taking 6 classes per semester at Housatonic. Surely this would be a breeze. Boy, was I wrong! I soon discovered that UConn, for whatever reason, didn't offer required classes for entire semesters at a time - with no notice of when they'd be offered again.

Confused and discouraged, I was left with only the hope of "someday" taking that Principles of Finance or Business Law class I needed. It was incredibly demotivating. As someone who loves plans and schedules, it crushed my enthusiasm and made it very difficult to stay motivated.

"Maybe I can take these classes at Housatonic and transfer them into UConn", I wondered. Good thinking, but unfortunately not possible. Like most universities, UConn has a strict "residency requirement" limiting number of transfer credits they will accept.

This is one of the biggest ways traditional colleges restrict your flexibility. Once you hit your transfer limit, the residency requirement kicks in, and all remaining coursework must be completed at that school - even if it would be less expensive or more convenient to earn them elsewhere.

Great.

Then there was the cost. As an in-state commuter, each semester cost between $3,000 and $4,000. Not bad - especially compared to private schools - but not cheap, either. I had no student debt to this point and I wanted to keep it that way.

Each night, on my hour-long commute to school, I pressed myself: what am I going to do about this?

As a self-employed writer and entrepreneur, I didn't technically "need" my degree yet. It wasn't holding me back in any immediate way. But it mattered to me nonetheless. I had spent the last few years reversing a lifetime of scholastic failure. I was proud of my A's, proud of my Dean's List awards and proud of how far I'd come. Finishing my bachelor's was the final chapter in my academic turnaround...and the system was doing everything in its power to make me wait for it!

Sometimes it was too demoralizing to think about. I went through brief episodes of denial, telling myself that I would "somehow" be able to pay without borrowing or "somehow" take the courses UConn wasn't offering. It was all I could do for a few moments of relief in a seemingly hopeless situation.

But when I came to my senses, I knew that was total BS. There was no "somehow." Either I could afford it or I couldn't. Either the classes were available or they weren't. The gods of wish fulfillment were not going to munificently protect me from hard numbers or school policy. It was time to be brutally honest with myself. If I stayed at UConn, I'd pay a ton of money and probably wait two more years to graduate. What I needed was a solution: a realistic plan that acknowledged these sad facts and strategically overcame them.

All options were on the table: alternative degree programs, different schools, even a new major, if it would help me graduate faster.

The solution I discovered, the Do-It-Yourself Degree, is spelled out in the chapters that follow. I present a full year of intense research and personal discovery; plus a practical gameplan you can follow without confusion.

In short, I am going to show you how to "hack" college by earning your degree faster and for less money than you ever dreamed possible. You're going to get every ounce of relevant learning you would get in a classroom with a lot less hassle!

Chapter 2: The DIY Degree Approach In a Nutshell

My quest for a speedier graduation started out pretty aimlessly. I searched Google for things like "get my degree faster" and "faster ways to get college credit" - anything that seemed relevant to what I was trying to do.

Most of what I found was totally worthless. Scams, diploma mills, shady online colleges and all the usual garbage that discouraged me from looking into this sooner. But persistence paid off, and a few hours in, I found an article by Josh Kaufman, author of The Personal MBA.

The title - **How To Get An Accredited Undergraduate Degree in 1 Year For $4,000** - told me that I was in for a refreshingly straightforward discussion of this topic. Having read his excellent articles on entrepreneurship, I knew Josh wouldn't even be writing about this without practical, real-world advice to share.

I was right.

What Josh explained is that you can "test out" of a degree just like you can test out of a class. Most schools won't force you through a semester of College Algebra, for example, if a placement test says you're ready for Pre-Calculus. It's a great time-saver, but schools aren't eager to tell you about it. They'd rather you take College Algebra anyway, because it means you stay longer and spend more.

By using the approach Josh outlined, you can literally earn an *entire degree* this way. Instead of attending dozens of courses, you study on your own and take an exam for each subject. The exams Josh talks about (called CLEP exams) are affordable - around $77 apiece - and can be taken at virtually any college or testing center in the country.

Each one is worth 3-12 credits (depending on the exam.) Once you pass enough exams to obtain a degree - usually 120 credits for a bachelor's - you transfer them all to a distance learning school like Excelsior or Thomas Edison or Charter Oak. After paying their admissions/graduation fees, you become a graduate of that school and receive a real, regionally accredited bachelor's degree to proudly display on your resume.

There aren't exams for every single college subject...meaning that some majors might require you to take a handful of online courses in addition to your exams. But you can still earn the vast majority of your degree via testing.

No homework, no class attendance, no school bureaucracy or BS.

These schools aren't new. Busy adults have been earning degrees at these colleges with online courses for more than fifteen years. What IS new is the approach of earning your whole degree with EXAMS (which you take and study for at your own pace) rather than with coursework. Other colleges allow credit-by-examination as well, but usually with strict limits (for example, "maximum of 20 credits earned via examination.") These limits are put in place for the college's benefit as a way of forcing you to buy credits in the more expensive "classroom" format.

The schools I name have NO such limit, so you can earn your whole degree (or most of it – again, depending on major and test availability) with exams.

This article set my mind on fire. My frustration melted away, replaced by surging confidence and the knowledge that a solution was at hand.

Unlike UConn and most other schools, Excelsior has **no** residency requirement. I simply transferred all the credits I had earned so far, took exams for the ones I still needed, and earned my bachelor's degree in four months instead of two years.

Not That Simple

Josh's article on "hacking" a college degree was superb - I encourage you to read it for yourself, and it's spot-on as far as it goes. In fact, it single-handedly convinced me that this was doable. But there's only so much territory one article can cover. It soon dawned on me that there were lots of details which would only become clear once I clarified them:

- **Which** exams should I take?
- What **other** types of exams are there besides CLEP?
- How are those other types of exams **different** from CLEP?
- Which **order** should I take them in?
- Who do I call?
- How do I enroll?
- How do I choose a **degree program**? There are literally dozens.
- What subjects/credits are **required** for my degree?
- How do I actually **schedule** my exams?
- How do I know for sure that they're going to count toward MY degree requirements?
- Are there ways to earn credits quickly **OTHER** than exams?
- Once I pass an exam, how do I **notify** my school and make sure those credits get there?
- What if I **fail** an exam? Can I re-take it? **Should** I retake it? If so, when? If not, how do I earn credit for that subject?

- What's the difference between **upper and lower-level** credit?
- How do I **get** upper-level credit? Most CLEP exams are for lower-level credit only.
- Which exams are **graded** and which are **pass/fail**? How does that affect my **GPA**?
- Does my school accept [exam here] for [course requirement here]?
- What about college courses I've **already** taken? Will the school I enroll in count those credits toward my degree? How many? Which ones?
- How do I track my progress?
- **How long will all of this take?**

I love research more than breathing and gleefully wrestled ALL of these answers from course advisors, articles and web forums. I spent sleepless nights learning how some weirdo shaved three months off his degree schedule or got an edge on an exam I was studying for. I found it intellectually challenging to treat this approach like an experiment and search for ways to optimize it.

But I knew that most people didn't have time for that. They just wanted instructions, so they could earn their degree quickly and focus on what matters to them.

That's when I realized that **this** is what was missing from the alternative/online degree world. A clear-cut gameplan with explanations, timelines and action steps that lead to a degree on the other side.

That gameplan forms the rest of this book. For now, just know that the chart below contains each major step on your journey toward a DIY Degree. When you feel overwhelmed or demoralized, refer back to this chart. Take solace in where you are now, where the next step will take you and where you will ultimately be.

STEPS	COMPLETED?
Choose your distance learning school.	
Choose your degree program.	
Identify your **required** credits	
Select your **elective** credits	
Connect all required and elective credits to **exams** (or courses, if a few subjects lack exams)	
Decide **which order** to take those exams/courses in	
Fill out your **DIY Degree Gameplan** (included) with that schedule	
Validate your gameplan by asking an advisor to approve it in full	
Execute your gameplan by taking each exam/course in order	
Earn your degree!	

Each step of the process is explained in chapters to follow.

The rest of this e-book will teach you how to complete every step above and construct your own rapid graduation roadmap by yourself.

To watch over my shoulder as I build a fully fleshed-out degree plan, visit:

www.DoItYourselfDegree.com/watch-learn

Chapter 3:
What Is a "Real" Degree?

First, I want to clear up any lingering suspicions you might have about the DIY Degree approach. If you're as skeptical as I was, you want to be certain that you aren't staking your future on some hunt for fool's gold. And I want you to be confident about the decision you're making.

So let's talk about real degrees and fake degrees.

Say what you want about traditional colleges and universities. They may be slow, clumsy, and expensive, but one thing is guaranteed: their degrees are real. Employers will not question their legitimacy at all. Whether those degrees are as **valuable** as you think (in terms of actual earning power) is another story. What no one can deny is that you are receiving a degree people respect and recognize.

But what *is* a real degree, exactly?

This is an important question. After all: when you see those scammy-looking "online college" commercials, isn't this what you're worried about? Aren't you concerned that you might be handing money to a fly-by-night diploma mill for a credential no employer accepts?

Of course. The sales pitch sounds great, but for all you know, the degree won't be worth the paper it's printed on. And often times, that's exactly the case. It's incredibly easy for a scammer to masquerade as a degree-granting institution and sell you a worthless credential.

Shameless Example: InstantDegrees.com

InstantDegrees.com is as sleazy as it gets. Visitors to the website are greeted with a glowing orange menu of degrees they can buy as if they were ordering cheeseburgers from a McDonald's drive-thru.

I'm not kidding. Somewhere, a real human being thought he was buying a PhD for less than the monthly payment on a Honda Civic.

Online since **2001** - Now in our **10th** year!

100% Approval   No Coursework   100% Legal
Associate Degree. $120 USD
Bachelor Degree. $130 USD
Masters Degree. $155 USD
Doctorate Degree. $180 USD
Professorship. $210 USD
Fellowship. $210 USD
100% Approval   No Coursework   100% Legal
What is the quality like? (Example Graduation Package)
$180 USD of Career Boosting ebooks FREE with EVERY order

Order your Degree

No Coursework or Exams

14

It gets worse. Check out these gems from their FAQ section:

- You will be earning your degree through a "legal loophole" (how reassuring!)
- The degree you ~~buy~~ earn will be "legally accredited" (huh?...real degrees are REGIONALLY accredited, which I'll explain later)
- You cannot choose the institution you "graduate" from. Instead, it's chosen for you by InstantDegree.com's "experts" depending on which degree and subject you want
- You won't know the name of the college you're "graduating" from until AFTER paying, in order to "secure the confidentiality of the institution and the security of YOU, the client"
- Direct quote: "The act of making payment is a declaration that you have read and agree to be bound by the Terms of Service and that that the person named on the diploma has sufficient Life/Work Experience or Prior Study to justify the award. We then make an application to the College or University on your behalf in a way we know will be accepted."
- In other words: you just pay us and graduate, simply by SAYING you've studied. Riiiiight...

And get this! If you happen to be skeptical of some random website selling $200 degrees on the honor system, InstantDegrees.com has a special response for you. Here's what their FAQ says about "critics."

Critics. Why you should ignore them

You must not forget that your degree is obtained by exploiting legal loopholes.

Critics have NO LEGAL argument. Our security protocols reduce the probability and impact of negative publicity, but we cannot remove the threat altogether. In the event that the institution you have graduated from is the target of such comments you should frankly, ignore it. Opinions of this nature (usually made anonymously or by people with very questionable histories involved in non-traditional degree granting institutions) carry NO legal weight whatsoever.

In the final analysis, what REALLY counts is the LEGALITY of the degree and NOTHING ELSE. So long as you have not misused or misrepresented your degree in violation of the FAQ and TOS you have NOTHING to fear.

The very reason that you are here is because you want to avail yourself of the positive social engineering possibilities of a legally granted degree. In that action you have proved yourself smarter than BOTH the average citizen with no degree AND smarter than the so-called academics.

These are people who have frittered away years in classrooms absorbing blindly and thoughtlessly second hand information in a theoretical environment completely removed from real life, and for what? In order to acquire the right to use the same Title or post-nominal letters that you can legally acquire in a matter of days for the price a meal in a decent restaurant.

Who is really smarter?

You are the one called to the front of the queue in airports; you are the one getting the free upgrade to first class; you are the one sitting at the good table not too near the band overlooking the river; you are the one dazzling your future employers with your skills and abilities at an interview rather than having your Résumé ditched by a computer programmed to scan all applications and send rejection slips to perfectly capable applicants who happen not to have a degree; The benefits are endless.

The degrees available thru us are obtained thru the exploitation of legal loopholes, but legally that does not make them of any less worth of a "worked for" degree.

In the final analysis, the LEGALITY of a degree is ALL that LEGALLY matters."

I wish I were making this up, but I'm not. You can visit InstantDegrees.com right now, click "FAQ" and scroll directly to the quote I just showed you.

Let's pause for a reality check

I'm all for beating the system. I often refer to the DIY Degree as a way to "hack" college, for example. But if you believe websites like InstantDegree.com, you need your head examined. A degree is not simply bought. It is earned. Whether you earn it by passing exams or by completing courses, you are going to work for it. You can work *smarter* (using tactics and strategies to cut down on completion time) but there is no escaping the necessity of at least SOME work.

Also, consider InstantDegree.com's response to critics. It might sound impressive, yet if you read carefully, you'll notice a total lack of facts or arguments. It's just one intellectually dishonest debate tactic after another, including:

- **Questioning the motives of the opponent** (claiming that anyone who criticizes them is "anonymous" or has a "very questionable history")
- **Arousing envy** (being first in line, dazzling future employers, etc.)
- **Stereotyping** (insulting "the average citizen" and "so-called academics")
- **Claiming privacy with regard to claims about self** (refusing to disclose WHICH schools they work with until after payment, because of "confidentiality")
- **Ill-defined words** (repeatedly saying their degrees are "legal" without saying how, why, or for what purposes)
- **Citing irrelevant facts or logic** (suggesting that because their degrees are "legal" they are somehow on equal footing with those issued by regionally accredited colleges or universities)
- **Mockery** (ridiculing people who have "wasted their time" earning degrees with coursework or exam completion)
- **Playing on widely-held fantasies** (telling readers they can have the same thing that others worked hard for "in a matter of days for the price of a meal in a decent restaurant")
- **Straw man** (attacking generic, nameless "critics" rather than refuting a SPECIFIC opposing point of view - such as the one I'm about to lay out below.)

(There are probably more that I missed. Check out John T. Reed's terrific list of intellectually honest and dishonest debate tactics here: **http://www.johntreed.com/debate.html**)

I wrote this chapter because InstantDegrees.com could not be more wrong. They say the "legality" of a degree is all that matters, but legality is is only part of the story. Just because it's legal for a company to sell you something they *call* a degree doesn't mean employers will *recognize* it as one.

Let's be clear on precisely what a "real" degree is

It's not a handshake agreement between colleges and employers. The company you'll work for someday won't "just know" that a degree from XYZ State University is legitimate. It's about one thing, and one thing only:

Accreditation. Specifically, *regional* accreditation.

What regional accreditation means is that the school you go to (its facilities, leadership, curriculum and teaching standards) has been "checked out" and approved by educational accreditation bodies. Every school you have ever attended - all the way back to elementary - is only allowed to operate because they are accredited in this manner.

Here's how Wikipedia defines regional accreditation:

> "...the process by which one of several educational accreditation bodies, each serving one of six defined geographic areas of the country, accredits schools, colleges, and universities. Each regional accreditor encompasses the vast majority of public and nonprofit private educational institutions in the region it serves. They accredit (and therefore include among their membership) nearly all elementary schools, junior high schools, middle schools, high schools, and public and private institutions of higher education that are academic in nature."

There are six regional accreditation bodies across America. Each one accredits educational institutions within the states it presides over. A list of all six can be found on Wikipedia.

Virtually all colleges you can name are regionally accredited. Every state school, every community college and most private universities.

In this book, I discuss three distance-learning colleges: Excelsior College, Thomas Edison State College and Charter Oak State College. **All** of them are regionally accredited. Excelsior and Thomas Edison by the *Middle States Association of Colleges and Schools* (MSA) and Charter Oak by the *New England Association of Schools and Colleges* (NEASC.)

Thus, their degrees are every bit as real as what you'd get from any other accredited school in New York, New Jersey and Connecticut. Columbia and Cornell are accredited by MSA. Yale is accredited by NEASC.

Excelsior graduates have gone on to attend Harvard, Dartsmouth and a whole list of other top graduate schools that I name in the next chapter.

Schools like Excelsior don't have the impressive *brand names* of their Ivy League counterparts, but they are accredited, recognized and endorsed by the same academic bodies. And they **don't involve any student debt at all**, never mind tens of thousands of dollars worth.

If you're not sure whether a college like Excelsior or Thomas Edison is legit, here's a quick way to find out. Visit **http://ope.ed.gov/accreditation/,** a Department of Education website that lets you verify the accreditation of any college.

To recap: when people refer to "real" colleges and degrees, what they actually mean is "regionally accredited." This is what employers, graduate schools and other organizations want to know about your degree. Is your college regionally accredited or not? If so, you have a "real" degree and there will no doubt about its merit. If not, you were sold something other than the real thing.

What about national accreditation?

It's better than no accreditation at all, but still not as strong. While nationally accredited organizations are not necessarily "scams", it's really hit or miss.

The main difference is that regional accreditation is for *non-profit* schools while national accreditation (for the most part) applies to *for-profit* schools. When a school is for-profit, people wonder if the school is more concerned with high academic standards or admitting as many students as possible. Trade schools tend to be nationally accredited, for example. Their certifications are typically less valuable than degrees from regionally accredited colleges.

This key ingredient - regional accreditation - is what you need to look for. Scammy websites will reassure you that their degrees are "legal" but that's beside the point. As I said earlier: just because it's legal for them to sell you something they CALL a degree doesn't mean employers will ACCEPT it as one.

Bottom line: If the college granting your degree *is not* regionally accredited, there will be doubts about its value. Doubt from jobs you apply for, doubt from graduate schools you wish to attend, doubt from anyone who knows anything about academics. Count on it.

That's why I built the strategies in this book around only the three colleges discussed above: Excelsior, Thomas Edison and Charter Oak.

(**Note:** These three are not the *only* regionally accredited distance-learning schools.)

Chapter 4: Picking Your Distance Learning School

The first step to obtaining a DIY Degree is selecting and enrolling in a distance learning school.

As noted in the last chapter, I focus on three in this book:

- **Excelsior College** (Albany, NY)
- **Thomas Edison State College** (Trenton, NJ)
- **Charter Oak State College** (New Britain, CT)

Here are their respective websites:

- **www.excelsior.edu**
- **www.tesc.edu**
- **www.charteroak.edu**

I chose these schools because they all:

- Are real, regionally accredited colleges with .**edu** addresses
- Have no residency requirement (meaning they allow unlimited test-out)
- Accept transfer credits from most legitimate schools
- Possess strong reputations in academia
- Operate primarily over the web

Because these colleges operate primarily over the web, you do not need to live in their states to attend.

For purposes of this book, we will be focused primarily on **Excelsior College**. Since I obtained my degree there and have first-hand experience with the school, that is the one I am most comfortable advising you on. I want to give you SPECIFIC advice, suggestions and action steps that I know for a fact will work. So if you notice me talking about Excelsior in each chapter, it's not because I'm a paid spokesman for the school. It's just because that's the school I know best.

However, the DIY Degree approach IS applicable at any other school that meets the same criteria.

Facts About Excelsior College

Since you've purchased this book and read this far, I want to pause and tell you about the college you'll soon be graduating from. Here's a brief summary of the school's history from their website:

> Excelsior College was founded in 1971 by the New York State Board of Regents, and was originally known as the Regents External Degree Program (REX). Initial development of the College was funded by major grants from the Ford Foundation and the Carnegie Corporation. From 1971 until 1998, Regents College (as it became known in 1986) operated as a program of the Board of Regents (which also served as its board of trustees) and under the authority of The University of the State of New York by which degrees and diplomas were awarded during that period.

In April 1998, the Board of Regents granted the College a charter to operate as a private, nonprofit, independent institution and on January 1, 2001, Regents College changed its name to Excelsior College. Today, an independent board of trustees governs Excelsior College and it is comprised of prominent individuals in the fields of education, business, and the professions from across the United States.

In recent years, Excelsior has become a top choice among military personnel who wish to continue their studies while stationed abroad. Excelsior also claims to be the largest educator of nurses in the United States.

Here are some additional facts from Excelsior's website:

Excelsior at a Glance

- 27 *flexible* degree programs
- 8 credit-bearing certificate programs
- 136,000+ graduates to date
- 30,000 enrolled students
- Largest educator of nurses in the United States

Student Diversity

- Average age: 38
- More than 30% are from groups historically underrepresented in higher education
- More than 30% are active-duty or reserve military personnel
- More than 85% reside outside our home state of New York

Mail:
Excelsior College
7 Columbia Circle
Albany, NY 12203-5159

Phone:
888-647.2388

You can learn more about Excelsior on the web at
www.excelsior.edu.

If you want to request more information, visit the school's
website. I encourage you to do that. Although I want you to get
your degree quickly, this is your future we're talking about. You
should feel totally comfortable and confident before deciding to
move forward with a DIY Degree.

Here's what their information packet will look like

Top grad schools that accept Excelsior students

What finally convinced me to enroll at Excelsior was the list of top institutions who have accepted their graduates in the past. According to their student handbook, Excelsior graduates have gone on to earn advanced degrees at such well-known graduate schools as:

- Harvard University
- Yale University
- Columbia Law School
- Cornell University
- Michigan State
- Northwestern University
- Pennsylvania State University
- Rutgers University
- Temple University
- University of California, Berkeley
- Villanova University
- John Hopkins University

As someone who once wanted to attend Harvard Business School this was very re-assuring.

How to enroll

You don't technically need to enroll at Excelsior before taking exams, but I recommend doing so. As an enrolled student, you can automatically have your exam scores sent to Excelsior for free. If you take your exams first and enroll later, you may have to pay a fee to send all your scores to the school. (Not to mention the possible logistical headache of manually sending 30-40 exam scores and making sure they all get there.)

The enrollment application is quick and easy:

Apply online: **http://www.excelsior.edu/admissions**

The application fee is **$75**, whether you apply online or mail your application in. If you apply online, you'll need to use a credit card. If you apply by mail, you can use check or money order payable to "Excelsior College."

You can also fax your application to Excelsior at **518-464-8700** (though your transcripts still need to be sent via mail.) Remember: you don't have to go to Excelsior if you don't want to. This enrollment process is roughly the same no matter which distance-learning school you decide to attend.

Costs & financing

Aside from the application fee, there is an **$895** fee to enroll in Excelsior's "multi-source" option. This is the one you want, as it means you are not required to take any courses through Excelsior. (Remember, you'll be earning your entire degree with exams.)

Luckily, you can spread this $895 out over a flexible payment plan. I was able to split the amount into six payments of about $160 per month. **The payment plan will be offered to you when you enroll online after being accepted.** Your acceptance letter will tell you exactly where to go to do that.

There is also a **$495** graduation fee which you pay after completing all of your exams. Don't worry about this for now - focus on the steps ahead.

What if I have credits from another college?

If you've already taken courses at another college, chances are your new distance learning school (Excelsior or otherwise) will accept them. This is extremely helpful, because any credits you've already earned can accelerate your graduation. What you need to do is obtain an OFFICIAL COPY of your transcripts from whatever school you went to.

Note that "official copy" means a sealed envelope that you send to Excelsior or your school of choice UNOPENED. My suggestion: if you have transcripts to send, apply by mail so that your application and transcripts arrive at the school in one envelope.

Here's exactly what you need to say at your school

Just go to the registrar's office and say the following:

> "Hi, I'm transferring to another college and need an official copy of my transcripts to send them. I'm going to mail it to them myself, along with my transfer application. Can you please print up an official copy of those for me?"

Some schools will take a couple of weeks to do this for you. Others will print them up right away. My advice is to put this book down right now and get the process underway. It will take Excelsior 2-4 weeks to evaluate your transcripts, so the sooner you send them, the sooner you'll know if Excelsior accepts your credits. If the school is nearby, go in person rather than e-mailing so you can be sure a real person is taking care of it.

After the school reviews your transcripts, you'll receive an email about which ones were accepted (as well as which ones still need to be earned.)

Note: If you have no prior college experience and are getting your entire degree the DIY way, you won't have any transcripts. Instead, include a copy of your high school diploma or GED with the enrollment application.

What about the "Degree Selection Information" section of the application?

This is where you pick the degree program that you're applying for. It's a critical step, and I devote the entire next chapter to it. Once you finish reading it (and make your decision) you can check the appropriate box on that section of the application and mail everything in.

Here's where to mail your application and transcripts

Excelsior College
Office of Registration and Records
7 Columbia Circle
Albany, NY 12203-5159

If you have questions at any time during the application/admissions process

Call **888-647-2388**, ext. 27 or e-mail **admissions@excelsior.edu**. If you opt to attend a different distance-learning school, use the appropriate helplines or email addresses at that college.

Chapter 5:
Choosing Your Degree Program

Before you apply, you need to choose a degree program.

I want to slow down here and spend some time on this, because degree choice is such a controversial and touchy subject. And since most students do an absolutely terrible job of this (for reasons explained below) I want to arm you with a strong intellectual framework for making a smart decision.

We all know that college students (as a group) are notoriously indecisive about their majors. MSNBC summed up the problem back in 2005:

> "Ask young children what they want to be when they grow up and the answer will change three times before dinner. Ask them when they are 18 and the answer is unlikely to be any more decisive.
>
> Eighty percent of college-bound students have yet to choose a major, according to Dr. Fritz Grupe, founder of MyMajors.com. But they are still expected to pick schools, apply to and start degree programs without knowing where they want to end up. It is little wonder 50 percent of those who do declare a major, change majors — with many doing so two and three times during their college years, according to Grupe."

Even more troubling, according to the College Board, is that five and six year students are not uncommon. In fact, "roughly 40% of those who start a four-year degree program have still not earned one after year six."

Now, it's easy to ridicule these students for being "wishy-washy." But let's look past the surface. Sure, a healthy percentage of these students are just prolonging adolescence and paying little mind to their futures. But not ALL of them are. A great number of students are earnestly trying to select the best major and simply failing at it.

Why?

The number one reason, I suspect, is that they're rushing the decision and making it with criminally scarce information. The typical 18 year-old lacks the self-knowledge and life experience needed to predict their career path and select a degree program in line with their passions. Many older adults are no surer of these questions than late teens are.

Absent this wisdom, students are left with peer pressure ("Don't you want a high-paying job?") glossy course descriptions ("I guess psychology/business/English sounds cool") or, worst of all, student debt anxiety ("I need to pay off these loans somehow") as their only guideposts.

Is it any surprise that degree programs chosen this way are abandoned after a half-hearted semester or two of coursework? Or that most adults wind up in careers with no connection to their majors?

The surprising irrelevance of your major

Now that I've thoroughly depressed you, here's the good news: it probably doesn't matter what your major is.

I know it sounds crazy, but for 90% of people, it's really, actually true. Here's why.

Despite common beliefs, colleges are not technical schools and a degree program isn't career training. The employer who eventually hires you (assuming you choose to work for others) won't care that you took Intermediate Algebra or Abnormal Psychology. Your coursework, in the grand scheme of things, is basically irrelevant.

This goes straight to the heart of why degrees have become so important in the last thirty years. Something like 70% of jobs now require at least an associate's degree (and that number is rising every year.) Why do employers value degrees so much? If they aren't synonymous with hard, usable knowledge, what's the point?

My best friend's father (a senior project manager at Pitney-Bowes) once heard his son and I complain about how "useless" college material is and set us straight. What he told us (and what many never realize) is that *college is not job training.* No – what an undergraduate degree demonstrates is that you can finish what you start. A four-year program of study may not contain job-specific material, but it does prove that you're responsible and at least minimally competent.

That's why, if you pay attention, so many job descriptions say "bachelor's degree in [subject] OR EQUIVALENT." That's code for "if you can sell me on why your degree is relevant, the job is yours."

I'll show you an example. Let's say you majored in psychology, but had a change of heart and now want to work in marketing. You've been studying independently and really believe this is the career for you. Here's what you would say during the interview when your degree is brought up:

"Well sir or mam, I know the job calls for a business major, but I actually believe my psychology degree is equally or even more useful in this position. After all, fundamentally, what IS marketing? It's psychology (understanding the motivations of customers) and math (tracking the performance of ad campaigns). I'm oversimplifying to an extent, but with a little training, I know I can use my psychology education to reach your company's marketing goals."

Who could possibly say no to that? Sure, you might get "By-The-Book Joe" as your interviewer, who says no just to honor company policy. But over two, three, four or more interviewers, you WILL get someone who sees the value in your degree and hires you for the job you want.

Of course, what I'm saying here isn't true 100% of the time. If you want to be research chemist or an accountant, you can't slide into those careers with a slick explanation about your English degree. Someone hell-bent on a very strict career path ought to do things by the book. But if you're undecided about your future and just want to get a bachelor's degree behind you, it's way better to get a degree - any degree - and worry about positioning it later.

Tips for choosing a degree program

Picking a degree program is very personal and there's only so many hard-and-fast rules I can offer. However, after years of experience with both traditional and distance-learning colleges (plus work experience spanning entrepreneurship, freelancing and "regular jobs") I do have some general guidelines:

- **Pick broad over specific.** A broad degree is a versatile degree. Marketing, psychology, business, economics: all of these subjects cover vast amounts of territory, which lets you argue that your degree applies to nearly any job available. Conversely, a degree in theater or classic literature paints you into a corner. Unless you're dead set on working in those fields, you may find it difficult to branch out if your interests or passions change. Which, as I showed earlier, they almost certainly will.

- **Pick a degree you can fully (or almost fully) test out of.** Right now, business degrees can be tested out of 100%. Degrees like psychology, accounting, and liberal arts can be "mostly" tested out of: say, 80% or 85% test-out and 10% or 15% online courses. Helpfully, these degrees are also more broad than specific, satisfying that criteria.
- **Study what you like, not what you'd like to like.** On the other hand, there's a lot to be said for following your heart. Think about what you selfishly enjoy, what you would study and find fascinating even if you had to do it as a hobby. You're way more likely to stay committed to a degree that taps into these passions than to one you chose solely for its expected future salary. Most degrees (and professions) fail this test. As Paul Graham asked, "how many corporate lawyers would do their current work if they had to do it for free, in their spare time, and take day jobs as waiters to support themselves?"
- **Ignore your friends.** They mean well (sometimes) but chances are, your friends aren't basing their opinions on research. They're just speculating and listening to the sounds of their own voices. Most people who boldly declare which major you should choose do not even know what's in this chapter, never mind what's best for you ten or twenty years into the future.

- **Stick with it.** The reason I want you to focus so much on picking a good degree program is so that you'll stick with it once you do. Constantly changing degree programs is the fastest way to be stuck in school forever.

With all of this in mind, it's time to make a choice. Go to **Excelsior.edu** and click on the "Programs" tab.

There, you will find a complete listing of every degree program the school offers. Click on each one you're interested in for a "Program at a Glance" overview of that degree. From that screen, you can click the "Degree Chart" link (explained in detail in the next chapter) to see which credits are required for that degree.

If you are attending a distance learning school other than Excelsior, find the equivalent section of their website.

Huge benefit of the DIY Degree approach: flexibility

Despite what you've learned in this chapter, you may still decide to change your degree program at some point in the future. It would be naive of me to think otherwise. Luckily for you, flexibility is a huge benefit of the DIY Degree approach! Because you're financing your degree one inexpensive exam at a time (rather than with a massive, irreversible student loan) you can change course without incurring a huge expense.

Contrast that with the typical public or private university student, who, (upon deciding that engineering isn't for him), feels pressured to stick with it so he can graduate on time and repay his loans.

With the DIY Degree, a change of heart won't bankrupt you.

Chapter 6:
Identifying Your Required Credits

Now that you've chosen a degree program, we can begin getting into the nuts and bolts of the DIY Degree.

It's here that your college experience will begin to radically diverge from most other students. Typically, a student is shuffled through school with minimal guidance and permitted to take whatever courses they want, whether they'll count toward a degree or not.

In a certain sense, this is great. After all, college isn't just about racing to earn a degree. There's real value in self-exploration and taking classes solely for personal curiosity or intrigue. My 2009 philosophy class may not have added any practical value to my career, but I reflect on it almost every day. So I'm not here to dismiss experimentation.

However, at a certain point, enough is enough. While there's a lot to be said for freedom and choice, there's also a lot to be said for structure and commitment. Studies are increasingly showing that having more choices can be DEMOTIVATING. That's right - having more options to choose from can actually overwhelm us, until we give up and don't pick ANY.

My favorite blog, *The Art of Manliness*, summarizes one of these experiments:

"In a high end grocery store, tables offered customers a chance to sample either 24 or 6 different jams. Shoppers were offered a dollar off coupon if they bought a jar. The table with 24 jams attracted a bigger crowd than the 6 jams table, but people ended up tasting about the same number of jams at each. The big difference was in how many of the samplers were converted into customers; only 3% of people at the 24 jams table bought a jar, while 30% of the samplers at the 6 jar table bought a jar.

What's going on here? Why did increasing the number of choices actually decrease people's ability to make a decision?"

This is especially prevalent on college campuses. Many students want to complete their studies and earn a degree, but they aren't given a clear path. Course completion sheets are notoriously confusing (see the opening chapter of this book for the one I was given at UConn.) And let's be honest: colleges have a vested interest in creating this confusion. Like any other business (and make no mistake, higher education IS a business) they want you to stay in the "store" for as long as possible by taking as many classes as they can sell you.
You might say that's cynical, but ask yourself: does it matter more whether something is cynical, or whether it's true?

This is a major reason why so many students are on year five or six of a four-year degree. They spent so much time on unnecessary or irrelevant courses that they still haven't completed their required ones.

Enough.

In this chapter, we're going to analyze the "Degree Chart" of your degree program and determine exactly what your required courses are. Then, in the next chapter, we're going to determine your electives. Finally, in the chapter that follows, we're going to find exams for ALL of these courses and lay out a schedule for taking every one of them.

In this way, the DIY Degree approach contains no wasted motion. You can choose to study other subjects, of course, if you have genuine interest in them. But there will be no uncertainty whatsoever about which credits are NEEDED in order to earn your degree.

Required courses for Excelsior's General Business bachelor's degree

For demonstration purposes, we'll be analyzing Excelsior's General Business bachelor's degree. This is the degree I obtained, so it's the one I can most clearly make an example out of.

We'll start by looking at the Excelsior's "Degree Chart" for this degree.

Excelsior College   School of Business & Technology

DEGREE REQUIREMENTS CHART

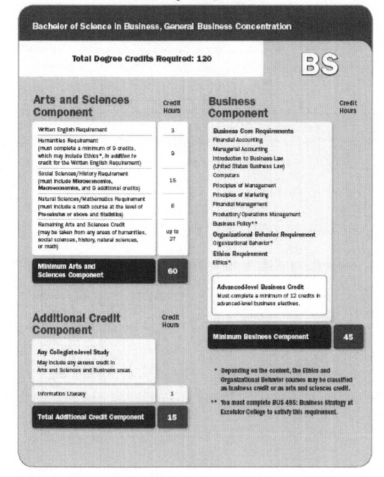

Bachelor of Science in Business, General Business Concentration

Total Degree Credits Required: 120

BS

Arts and Sciences Component

	Credit Hours
Written English Requirement	3
Humanities Requirement (must complete a minimum of 9 credits, which may include Ethics*, in addition to credit for the Written English Requirement)	9
Social Sciences/History Requirement (must include Microeconomics, Macroeconomics, and 9 additional credits)	15
Natural Sciences/Mathematics Requirement (must include a math course at the level of Precalculus or above and Statistics)	6
Remaining Arts and Sciences Credit (may be taken from any areas of humanities, social sciences, history, natural sciences, or math)	up to 27
Minimum Arts and Sciences Component	**60**

Additional Credit Component

	Credit Hours
Any Collegiate-level Study May include any excess credit in Arts and Sciences and Business areas.	
Information Literacy	1
Total Additional Credit Component	**15**

Business Component

	Credit Hours
Business Core Requirements Financial Accounting Managerial Accounting Introduction to Business Law (United States Business Law) Computers Principles of Management Principles of Marketing Financial Management Production/Operations Management Business Policy**	
Organizational Behavior Requirement Organizational Behavior*	
Ethics Requirement Ethics*	
Advanced-level Business Credit Must complete a minimum of 12 credits in advanced-level business electives.	
Minimum Business Component	**45**

* Depending on the content, the Ethics and Organizational Behavior courses may be classified as business credit or as arts and sciences credit.

** You must complete BUS 495: Business Strategy at Excelsior College to satisfy this requirement.

For now, let's focus on the "Business Component." These are the credits that are absolutely required in order to earn this degree. The "Arts & Sciences Component" requires you to earn credits in courses of your choosing, which we'll get to in the next chapter.

As you can see, there are 11 required courses in this component:

- Financial Accounting
- Managerial Accounting
- Intro to Business Law
- Computers
- Principles of Management
- Principles of Marketing
- Product/Operations Management
- Business Policy
- Organizational Behavior
- Ethics

In addition to these required "core" classes, you are also required to complete 12 credits in "advanced-level" business courses. By "advanced-level", Excelsior means "upper-level." Don't be confused - it's actually a very simple distinction.

The difference between lower-level and upper-level credit

All the classes you take in college (whether it's at a traditional university or the DIY way) are classified as lower-level or upper-level. A lower-level course, generally speaking, is one taken by students in their first or second year of school. English Composition, Intro to Psychology, Algebra, Spanish 1 & 2 and Western Civilization are all typically lower-level courses.

An upper-level course, meanwhile, is one taken by students in their third or fourth year of school. They are meant to be harder and cover advanced, degree-specific material. Principles of Finance, Philosophical Issues in Bioethics, Human Resource Management and Research Methods in Psychology are examples of upper-level courses.

For our purposes, just know that "advanced-level credit" means "upper-level credit." The full exam list in the next chapter tells you which exams count for lower-level and upper-level credit.

With this degree in particular, you need 12 advanced-level BUSINESS courses. Be mindful of that when laying out your DIY Degree gameplan later on.

For now, just know that each and every one of the 11 courses in that bulleted list is REQUIRED. Meaning you will not get your degree without completing all of them.

NOTE: If you decided to attend Thomas Edison State College, Charter Oak or another distance learning school, they will all have similar degree breakdowns and lists of requirements. I'm using Excelsior in my examples because that's where I went and I know exactly how the process works there. You don't have to, though. Just adapt the process to the school you're attending.

Chapter 7:
Selecting Your Elective Credits

In the last chapter, we figured out what your required courses are. In this one, we'll select your Arts & Sciences (also known as "elective") credits.

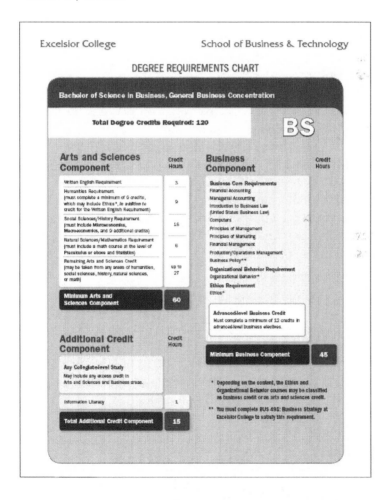

Once again, we'll use the General Business bachelor's degree as our example. (Remember, though: ANY degree program you choose should have a Degree Requirements Chart like this one.)

Immediately, several things jump out at us. First, the Written English requirement. That's simple: there's a CLEP exam for English Composition.

Then, the Social Sciences requirement. This includes both microeconomics and macroeconomics, which make up 6 credits. But you also need 9 other credits in the Social Sciences.

What exams will you take to earn them? It's up to you. A full list of all the exams that are available, who offers them, how many credits they're worth, and links to exam descriptions is given in the next chapter. For now, just know that you WILL need 9 credits - in addition to micro and macro - in this area to graduate.

Next, we see the Natural Sciences/Math requirement. For this degree, that includes (ugh) Statistics and at least Pre-Calculus. (Luckily for you, I provide a super-easy way to earn math credits in the next chapter.) Note that for a different degree program, other courses might be required for this section. Biology or chemistry, for example.

Moving on, we come to Remaining Arts & Sciences credits, which you need 27 of in total. This is where you have the most flexibility of all. You get to choose from pretty much ANY subjects in humanities, social sciences, natural sciences, history or math. In the next chapter, I offer guidance on how to pick exams that satisfy these requirements and are easy to pass.

Finally, at the very bottom, we see the Additional Credit Component. This is another catch-all category where you basically get to earn 15 credits in whatever you want. Again: be strategic about which exams you choose. You'll learn more about this in the chapter to follow.

Of course, if you don't mind taking your time and aren't concerned with speed above all else, the Remaining Arts & Sciences credits are an opportunity to explore subjects you're genuinely interested in. The next chapter, again, contains a full list of all possible exam topics to pick from.

Chapter 8: Connecting All Requirements & Electives To Exams

With your course requirements (both core and arts & sciences) clarified, we come to my favorite part of the DIY Degree: connecting all of these credits to exams, so you can earn them without taking classes.

Remember: some majors MIGHT require you to take a small handful of courses in subjects that simply don't have exam options. Don't let this distract you from the bigger picture and the still-massive savings you will reap by earning your degree MOSTLY through testing.

This is what so many people don't believe (or realize) is possible. But in this chapter, you'll learn all about the credit-by-examination method: who offers these exams, what's on them, how to schedule them, and the finer points of what I like to call "exam strategy."

First, let's revisit what this approach is all about

Typically, people earn college credits by taking courses - either online or, more commonly, in person. For all the benefits of this approach (ability to ask questions, interaction with other students, group learning, etc.) it is incredibly costly and time-consuming. The beauty of the credit-by-examination method is that you can earn the exact same credits you WOULD have gotten by going to class...by taking exams instead.

In other words: rather than attending a semester's worth of English or Accounting or Psychology, you can simply study on your own, schedule exams at a local testing center, pass, and get your credits that way - without ever stepping foot inside a classroom. All on YOUR schedule, not a college's.

Now, before we dive in, the question I always answer when explaining this is, "WHICH exams?" So let's cover that first. On the next pages, I've laid out quick descriptions of the different types of exams you can take: who offers them, how they work, what they cost, and how to schedule them.

CLEP Exams

What: CLEP (College Level Examination Program) exams are offered by the College Board, who also administers the SATs. Spanning 33 subjects (from English Composition to Biology to Accounting) CLEP exams count for lower-level credit and are intended to test you on a semester's worth of knowledge in a given subject.

Each exam is approximately 90 minutes long, and, except for College Composition, is made up primarily of multiple-choice questions. Some exams do include other types of questions or optional essays.

Where: CLEP exams can be taken at virtually any nearby college or testing center. Visit this URL (**https://clep.collegeboard.org/search/test-centers**) to find testing sites in your area. When you find one, simply call the number provided and say "Hi, I'm calling to schedule a CLEP exam for [subject here] on [the date you want.] Could you please transfer me to the appropriate person or department?"

While taking the test (which are on the computer) you specify where you want your scores sent to (Excelsior) and they are automatically sent there after you finish. If you **fail** the exam, you won't be allowed to re-take it for 6 months.

Cost: $77 per exam, paid by debit or credit card at the test site

Visit (**https://clep.collegeboard.org/exam**) for more information about CLEP exams.

DSST Exams

What: DSST (DANTES Subject Standardized Tests) exams began as a Department of Defense initiative to help service members continue their educations. Today, they are administered by Prometric and available to civilians as well as military personnel. Content-wise, DSST exams are very similar to CLEP tests: 90 minutes, multiple choice, taken at testing centers.

The main difference is that while CLEP exams are for lower-level credit, DSST offers both lower-level and upper-level exams. There are 38 DSST exams in total, as of August 2011.

Where: DSST exams can be taken at virtually any nearby college or testing center. Pretty much anywhere that proctors CLEP exams will also proctor DSST exams. Use the URL above to find a testing center. When you find one, simply call the number provided and say "Hi, I'm calling to schedule a DSST exam for [subject here] on [the date you want.] Could you please transfer me to the appropriate person or department?"

While taking the test (which will be either on the computer or paper-and-pencil) you specify where you want your scores sent to (Excelsior or your school of choice) and they are automatically sent there after you finish. If you **fail** the exam, you won't be allowed to retake it for 3 months - better than the 6 month waiting period with CLEP tests, but still pretty significant.

Cost: $80 per exam, paid by debit or credit card at the test site

Visit (**http://getcollegecredit.com/**) for more information about DSST exams.

Excelsior College/UExcel Exams

What: Excelsior College exams are offered by Excelsior itself in various subjects. They are longer than CLEP or DSST exams - generally 3 hours and 130 multiple-choice questions. However, in my experience, they are not any harder than CLEP or DSST exams. UExcel is a partnership between Excelsior and Pearson VUE. The exams are basically the same as Excelsior College exams - they just cover different subjects.

Like DSST exams, some Excelsior College exams are lower-level credit and others are upper-level.

Since these exams are created and administered BY Excelsior, your scores automatically get sent to the school. If you **fail** the exam, you won't be allowed to retake it for 6 months.

Where: The only place you can take Excelsior College or UExcel exams are Pearson VUE testing centers, where you will be put through a security screening (fingerprints, photograph, video/audio monitoring, etc.) that resembles Fort Knox.

To take an Excelsior College exam, you must first register online at the following URL (**https://www.excelsior.edu** and click "Login") and then schedule a test date at a nearby Pearson VUE (**http://www.pearsonvue.com/excelsior/**) after receiving your "Permission to Test" letter in the mail.

Cost: $250 and up for Excelsior College exams, paid while registering on Excelsior's website. UExcel exams are $85.

Visit (**http://www.excelsior.edu/exams/choose-your-exam**) for more information about Excelsior College exams.

Thomas Edison State College Exams

What: Thomas Edison State College exams (also known as TECEPs) are a lot like Excelsior College exams. They are offered by Thomas Edison State College and cover various subjects that you may or may not need to earn your degree. Like DSST exams, some TECEPs are for lower-level credit and others are for upper-level.

Where: The logistics of taking TECEP exams are a little trickier than CLEPs and DSSTs, but not extremely difficult. Basically, you have two options. You can take your exam at Thomas Edison, which is in Trenton, NJ. Or if you live too far away for that, you can have Thomas Edison send a paper-and-pencil copy of your exam to a local library or college, who will then proctor the exam for you and send it back to Thomas Edison be scored.

Here are the exact emails to send.

First, send this to your local public library or college:

> SUBJECT: Can you proctor a college exam for me in [MONTH HERE]?
>
> Hi there,
>
> My name is _____. I'm emailing you today because I'd like to have someone from the library proctor an exam for me.
>
> Can you give me two or three possible dates for next month?

Also, please let me know the name and email address of whomever handles proctoring at the library, as I will need to inform Thomas Edison State College (the exam provider.)

I appreciate your fastest reply. Thanks!

Once the library or college replies, send the following email to "testing@tesc.edu."

SUBJECT: Can you send my TECEP exam to [NAME OF COLLEGE/LIBRARY] in [YOUR TOWN] for proctoring?

Hi there,

I recently registered for the [SUBJECT HERE] TECEP exam. I don't live in Trenton, though, so I'll need to have the exam proctored for me in [YOUR TOWN], where I live.

[PROCTOR HERE] from [NAME OF SCHOOL/LIBRARY HERE] has agreed to proctor for me next month. His email is [EMAIL HERE]. Can you please coordinate with him and confirm to me once you've mailed the test?

Please let me know. Thanks!

That's exactly what I did for my Operations Management exam. Thomas Edison was the only school (that I knew of) that offered an exam in that subject. However, in order to take it, I needed to have them send a copy to my local public library for proctoring. All I did was call the library, explain what I needed them to do and (once they said yes) told Thomas Edison where to mail the exam.

You then need to instruct Thomas Edison to send those scores to Excelsior, so that they go on your transcript and count for credit in that course.

Cost: $100, paid while registering on Thomas Edison's website. (This is a recent development: prior to June 2011, TECEP exams cost $500.)

Visit (**http://www2.tesc.edu/listalltecep.php**) for more information about Thomas Edison State College exams.

ALEKS Online Math Courses

What: ALEKS (**www.aleks.com**) is a website where students can take self-paced math courses on their computers. No one is watching or monitoring you. When you assess at 70% or higher on an assessment test, you are said to have "passed" the course.

Transferring your ALEKS credits to Excelsior (or your school of choice) after passing is a five-step process:

- Create an account at the American Council on Education credit registry. It's free and takes less than a minute: (**https://www2.acenet.edu/credit/?fuseaction=REGISTR ATION.main**)
- Next, log in with the account you created HERE: (**https://www2.acenet.edu/credit/?fuseaction=REGISTR ATION.main**)
- Then, click "Course Search" and enter in the information for the course you just passed:

- Click "Search" and the name of your course will appear below the search box:

Organization Name	Title	Course Number	ACE Course Nu...
ALEKS Corporation (McGraw Hill)	Introduction to Statistics		ALEK-0007

Search Results (1)

Click the course, and click "Add to transcript" on the screen to follow. It will then take 1-2 days for ALEKS to confirm that you did, indeed, pass that course.

- When you get the confirmation email from ACE that your credits were approved, log back into your ACE account. Now, instead of clicking "Course Search" like before, click "Order Transcripts." Follow the on-screen instructions to send a copy of your transcripts to your college. For Excelsior students, the address to use is:

Excelsior College
ATTN: Transcripts
7 Columbia Circle
Albany, NY 12203-5159

If you chose another school, you'll need to get the address from their website.

That's it. Just wait 1-2 weeks and your ALEKS math credits will show up on your Excelsior transcripts.

Where: ALEKS courses are taken online, at home, with no supervision whatsoever.

Cost: $20 per month. You sign up for a monthly subscription, take as many courses as you want, and end the subscription when you're finished. If you finish in the first month, you end the subscription and you paid $20 for however many credits you earned.

Visit (**www.aleks.com**) for more information about ALEKS online math courses.

What: Straighterline is a lot like ALEKS, only it costs a little more and offers classes in subjects other than math. A list of all Straighterline courses is provided in the DIY Degree Exam Master List.

Where: Straighterline courses are taken online, at home, without any supervision whatsoever.

Cost: $99 per month subscription. Other payment plans are available at Straighterline's website.

Visit (**www.straighterline.com**) for more information about Straighterline online courses.

Portfolio Learning Assessment

I've mentioned repeatedly that some classes lack an exam, requiring you to take the course in question to earn credit. Luckily, there is another option at your disposal for earning fast/convenient credit: Portfolio Learning Assessment.

PLA allows you to create a portfolio demonstrating college-level mastery of a specific subject. For instance, a self-taught computer programmer (rather than sitting through a four-month course in Object-Oriented Programming) could build a portfolio that includes a working, documented software application and earn credit that way instead.

PLA isn't quite as cheap as testing out, but it's still a lot less than coursework. Consider this HIGHLY worthwhile for subjects that lack an exam option.

Here is a massively detailed "how-to" post on PLA that I wrote for Personal MBA author Josh Kaufman:
http://joshkaufman.net/hacking-higher-education-moocs/

Actually doing it: selecting exams for all required credits

This is where the rubber meets the road. It's time to select which exams you'll take in order to satisfy your degree requirements.

To do that, please have the following three things in front of you:

- Your "Degree Overview" from Excelsior's website (or the school of your choice)
- The blank "Degree Gameplan" template included with this book
- The "DIY Degree Master Exam List" spreadsheet discussed above

Now, just start going down the list. For instance, no matter which degree program you picked, you're going to need English Composition. Looking at the "Exam List" spreadsheet, we see that the best fit for those credits is the College Composition CLEP exam. You could, alternatively, take the Excelsior College exam for English Composition, but it's way more expensive (as you can see from the descriptions above.) Therefore, it's better to take the CLEP exam. Go right on down the line and do this for all required classes.

I've included a sample "Degree Gameplan" for a General Business degree to show you what a completed one looks like. You don't need to get this exact degree, of course, but if you wanted to, you could literally use this gameplan exactly as written and earn it that way.

Is one exam better than another?

If you're asking whether colleges *prefer* certain exams, the answer is no. Credits are credits. All of these exams are legitimate credit sources, so it doesn't matter which ones you take.

What about difficulty? Are some exams harder than others?

Generally, no. I have not found CLEP exams to be easier than DSST (or vice-versa) or Excelsior exams to be trickier than TECEPs. Certain *subjects* are tougher than others, depending on your own knowledge and comfort level, but that's a given. The choice of which exam to take often comes down to COST, which I cover more below.

How do I study for these exams?

In the DIY Degree Exam Master List spreadsheet, I link to the "fact sheet" for each exam. These links include full topic breakdowns of what will be covered on the test. Don't worry about studying for now. I cover how to study in the last chapter.

Remember: to watch over my shoulder while I build a DIY Degree Gameplan
www.DoItYourselfDegree.com/watch-learn

Or, if you would like us to personally build a DIY Degree custom graduation roadmap FOR YOU, visit:
www.DoItYourselfDegree.com/done-for-you

Exam Strategy #1: Take cheaper versions of a subject exam FIRST

Always take the cheapest version of an exam first and aim to pass it. Think of the more expensive versions (Excelsior, TECEP, etc.) as "bullets in the chamber" - backup plans for if you fail the cheaper CLEP or DSST exams and don't want to wait to retake them.

EXAMPLES OF WHICH EXAMS TO TAKE AND WHEN:

If you need these credits:	Take this exam first:	Then this one if you fail:
English Composition	College Composition CLEP ($77)	English Composition TECEP ($100)
Intro to Psychology	Psychology CLEP ($77)	Psychology UExcel ($85)
Pre-Calculus	Pre-Calculus ALEKS ($20)	Pre-Calculus CLEP ($77)

Exam Strategy #2: Take 6 or 12 credit exams for rapid credit accumulation

There are also exams that count for 6 or 12 credits EACH. For example, the Spanish, French and German language CLEP exams each count for 12 credits. The Biology, Chemistry, Natural Sciences, Social Sciences & History all count for 6 credits each. A number of Excelsior College exams count for 6 credits as well.

The DIY Degree Exam Master List spreadsheet tells you how many credits each exam counts for.

Exam Strategy #3: Group similar exams together for rapid credit accumulation

As we covered in the last chapter (Arts & Sciences) you have significant leeway regarding which credits will satisfy these requirements. Same is true of the 12 "Advanced Business Credits" required for the General Business degree. Rather than being instructed to take specific classes, you are instead free to pick subjects for this part of your degree.

This is actually an incredible opportunity to be strategic and pick exams that are super-easy to pass.

Let me give you an example. For my degree (again, General Business) I was required to take Introduction to Business Law. After taking the Business Law CLEP, I thought to myself, "hmm...DSST offers a Business Law 2 exam. It counts for upper-level credit, which I need. And I bet the material is extremely similar to what I just studied."

It was. After two weeks of additional studying, I passed the Business Law 2 DSST with flying colors. In fact, had I known then what I know now, I would've studied for BOTH exams at the same time and taken them on the same day, rather than a month apart.

This is what the true DIY Degree masters do. I've encountered people who took two, three, sometimes four exams *in a single day* and walked out with 12 credits or more.

The point is, you can and should look for opportunities to do this. Look at your required credits, the ones you need regardless. Then, look at the "DIY Degree Exam List" spreadsheet and see if there are any similar exams that will count toward your degree. Chances are, you will find at least a few that do, and you can group these exams together for rapid credit accumulation.

MORE EXAMPLES OF SUBJECTS/EXAMS WITH SIGNIFICANT
OVERLAP:

If you already need:	Consider taking this, too:
Intro to Psychology	Intro to Sociology/Social Psychology/Intro to Educational Psychology, Human Growth & Development, etc.
Organizational Behavior	Human Resource Management, Labor Relations, etc.
Principles of Finance	Money & Banking, Financial Institutions & Markets, etc.
Intro to Computers	Management Information Systems

I would have earned my own degree a lot faster if I knew at the beginning what I know today. Just off the top of my head, I would've taken the Management CLEP, Psychology CLEP, Organizational Behavior ECE and Human Resource Management ECE in rapid succession, because there is significant overlap between these subjects.

Had I done that, I would've earned an entire semester's worth of credits in just a few weeks.

Because you have this book, you have that chance. You can strategically design your Degree Gameplan so that similar exams are taken in sequence and passed in way less time. TAKE ADVANTAGE OF THIS!

Exam Strategy #4: Use ALEKS online courses for fast, cheap math credits

I'm a pretty smart guy, but I'm terrified of math. Sadly, my degree **required** Statistics and Pre-Calculus in order to graduate. The idea of taking standardized tests in those subjects freaked me out like you wouldn't believe. "What am I going to do?", I thought to myself. I assumed I had hacked the degree process as far as possible and would simply need to grind these dreadful exams out.

Fortunately, that was not true. When it comes to math, the degree process CAN be hacked further. The answer: online math courses from **www.aleks.com**.

ALEKS was originally designed for colleges who wanted to offer supervised online math courses to their students. Today, however, it's possible for individual students (you) to sign up and take online courses at your own pace. No professor is supervising. You simply sign up for a $20/mo. account, select which course you want to take (ie, Principles of Statistics) and complete online exercises at your own pace.

Once you successfully complete at least 70% of the coursework, you generate an ACE transcript and send it to your college. (I covered this earlier in the chapter with step-by-steps and screenshots.)

That's what I did. I took both Statistics and Pre-Calculus through ALEKS (at my own pace), transferred them to ACE, and then to Excelsior. Credits earned, problem solved, no more advanced math for the rest of my life.

Plus, these ALEKS courses are pass/fail, so if you just barely pass by the skin of your teeth (like I did) it won't harm your GPA at all.

This is an even better deal for math geniuses. If you're a math whiz, you can literally sign up for ALEKS, assess at 70% or higher *in one day*, cancel your membership, and have your math credits for $20 (the first month's usage fee.) This could be the highest return on investment in all of higher education.

NOTE: Straighterline online courses serve the same purpose, but they are a bit more expensive. On the plus side, Straighterline offers courses in subjects other than math, providing a solid fallback option for if you fail a subject exam.

Exam Strategy #5: Be mindful of which exams are pass/fail and which are graded.

When you open the DIY Degree Exam Master List spreadsheet, you'll see that some exams are pass/fail while others are graded. This is a critically important distinction and yet another way for you to be strategic about which exams you take.

You may be familiar with the concept of Grade Point Average, or GPA. Your GPA is a numeric score that sums up your overall academic performance. The higher your GPA, the better you look to employers, graduate schools, or other interested parties. The lower your GPA, the worst you look.

Obviously, it's in your best interest to graduate with as high a GPA as possible. A 3.7 or 3.8 GPA will look phenomenal on your resume. But how do you get it? Luckily, the DIY Degree approach allows you to earn your credits in a way that maximizes your GPA. Very simply, you want to take subjects that you're **good** at for grades and subjects you're **bad** at for pass/fail. This way, your strengths are reflected in your GPA (by the fact that you earned A's) and your weaknesses are invisible. That's because pass/fail doesn't affect your GPA one way or the other. Even if you scrape by with a 70, your transcript will just say "PASS."

I did this for my math credits. I knew I would barely pass a Statistics or Pre-Calc course, so I earned those credits as pass/fail, using ALEKS courses.

Look at the DIY Degree "Exam List" spreadsheet. There, you'll see which exams are graded and which are pass/fail. You won't always be able to taking a subject you're **bad** at for a grade, but most of the time, you can and should.

Exam Strategy #6: Take easy exams first for quick wins and motivation

Whenever you begin a lengthy project or commitment, it's critical to get quick wins. A few early successes will show you that your goal is attainable and motivate you to keep moving. That's why I suggest taking exams that will be easy for you in the very beginning.

For example, I took the Marketing CLEP exam first, because I knew I would pass it effortlessly. But I saved the Principles of Finance DSST for last, because I knew studying for that would make me want to commit suicide every morning. Had I STARTED with that, I might have become demotivated and put off my next exam for weeks. By waiting until the end, I had the motivation of "once this is done, I'm ALL done."

How many exams should you schedule at one time?

Knowing which exams you're going to take is the first step. That's your DIY Degree gameplan. Next, you need to schedule them. This is a big decision: are you going to schedule one exam at a time? Or two or three? Or all of them? There are pros and cons to each approach. If you're nervous about giving yourself enough time to study (especially in the beginning) it might make sense to just schedule your first exam, pass it, and then think about the others.

I thought about doing it that way. What I soon realized, though, is how vulnerable this approach was to procrastination and avoidance. Without a schedule to keep me moving, I might just take comfort in my "plan" while doing nothing for weeks. (Hey, "know thyself" is the core of all wisdom...and I'm just as lazy as anyone else.)

Using psychology against yourself to study

That's why I advocate scheduling exams in batches. It's one thing to have a gameplan on a piece of paper. It's another to have five or six exam dates circled on your calendar that you see every morning. This changes your mindset, forcing you to prioritize studying and make sure you're prepared for the exams that are coming.

I also found it psychologically comforting to always have exams scheduled. Let's face it: earning a degree (whether at a traditional college or the DIY way) is a serious commitment. It takes time. Think about that old saying "idleness is the devil's playground." Think about why sitting around causes so many people to be depressed. Then think about how this applies to your degree.

Chances are, you won't push yourself month after month to keep scheduling one exam at a time. You'll be ever-aware of what that requires (studying, making time, etc.) and just put it off. But when you schedule 6 exams at a time, you don't have to push yourself. Your environment pushes for you!

Remember: the DIY Degree is a totally independent, self-managed approach. No one will urge you to work faster. You could spread these exams out over 10 years if you wanted to. But you bought this book to earn your degree QUICKLY. Don't forget that.

My personal rule of thumb was to allow 3 weeks between exams. In retrospect, that was too long. I found that it only took 7-10 days after an exam for me to be ready for the next one. Again: a lot of this is dictated by personal circumstance. Not everyone is as comfortable taking tests or has the same time availability. Do what works for you.

Look at your degree like an entrepreneur would

If this chapter makes it sound like you're "Frankensteining" your education, cobbling various exams and credit sources together to form a degree, you're right. That's exactly what you're doing. This might seem strange at first, but I encourage you to look at it differently.

We always see these studies about how much more college graduates earn in a lifetime than non-graduates. Here's one that I quickly Googled from a community college:

College Graduates Earn More

According to the United States Census Bureau, college graduates earn far more over their working lifetimes than non-college graduates. See the chart to the right.

- Every bit of education you get after high school increases the chances you'll earn good pay. Most college graduates earn a lot more money during their working years than people who stop their education at high school.
- The more education you get the more likely it is you will always have a job. According to one estimate, by the year 2028 there will be 19 million more jobs for educated workers than there are qualified people to fill them.

Education Level	Average Lifetime Earnings
Professional degree	$4.4 million
Doctoral degree	$3.4 million
Master's degree	$2.5 million
Bachelor's degree	$2.1 million
Associate's degree	$1.6 million
Some college	$1.5 million
High school graduate	$1.2 million
Non-high school graduate	$1 million

- Today most good jobs require more than a high school diploma. Businesses want to hire people who know how to think and solve problems.
- Education beyond high school gives you a lot of other benefits, including meeting new people, taking part in new opportunities to explore your interests, and experiencing success.

Source: Lorrain County Community College

Technically, these studies are accurate...but here's what they DON'T tell you. Simply earning a higher income doesn't mean you're better off. If you spend $100,000 for a degree (and take four years off to do it) you have incurred a huge opportunity cost.

You basically took out a loan against your future earnings, which must now be paid back over five, ten, maybe fifteen or twenty years. Even then, once all the loans are repaid and you've earned back all the income you lost by not working, YOU'VE JUST BROKEN EVEN.

You're back at square one. Then, after years of repaying loans and interest, you can start actually KEEPING the higher income you earned your degree for. Most college students don't realize this is what they've agreed to until after they graduate. They just see college as a magical guarantee of financial success. Yet, whether they realize it or not, their student loans often chain them to a life of indentured servitude.

The return on an investment is inversely proportional to the time and money invested. In plain English: the longer it takes you to earn a degree, and the more you pay for it, the less valuable it ultimately is.

The DIY Degree actually delivers what traditional universities promise

Fortunately, the reverse is also true. The less time it takes you to earn a degree, and the less you pay for it, the MORE valuable it ultimately is.

By earning your degree the DIY way, you are doing what so many students never do. You're being strategic. You're treating your degree as an investment, rather than a collegiate shopping spree. You're being efficient by extracting the *most value* for the *least cost*.

Consequently, you actually WILL reap the rewards of higher postgraduate income. Since you didn't take years off of work or incur costly student loans, all of that extra money goes straight into your pocket.

Remember: to watch over my shoulder while I build a DIY Degree Gameplan
www.DoItYourselfDegree.com/watch-learn

Or, if you would like us to personally build a DIY Degree custom graduation roadmap FOR YOU, visit:
www.DoItYourselfDegree.com/done-for-you

Chapter 9:
Sample DIY Degree Gameplan

In this chapter, I want to bring the DIY Degree approach down to earth by showing you a sample degree gameplan.

Assuming you wanted a bachelor's in General Business, you could follow this plan step-by-step, with no additional thinking or analysis, and obtain your degree. Just schedule these exams, study, pass each one, and you're done.

Not all of you will want this exact degree, of course. In that case, use the sample gameplan below as an example of how to create your own, rather than following this one verbatim.

Sample DIY Degree Gameplan For: Bachelor's in General Business

Note that each section of Excelsior's "Degree Overview" is accounted for below. If attending another school, this would need be modified.

Arts & Sciences Component (60 credits)

- College Composition Modular CLEP (3 credits)

- American Government CLEP (3 credits)

- Introductory Psychology CLEP (3 credits)

- Introductory Sociology CLEP (3 credits)

- Principles of Microeconomics CLEP (3 credits)

- Principles of Macroeconomics CLEP (3 credits)

- Social Sciences & History CLEP (6 credits)

- History of United States 1 CLEP (3 credits)

- Principles of Statistics ALEKS course (3 credits)

- Pre-calculus ALEKS course (3 credits)

- Ethics in America CLEP (3 credits)

- History of United States 2 CLEP (3 credits)

- Western Civilization 1 CLEP (3 credits)

- Western Civilization 2 CLEP (3 credits)

- Biology CLEP (6 credits)

- Humanities CLEP (6 credits)

- Human Growth & Development CLEP (3 credits)

Business Component (45 credits)

- Financial Accounting CLEP (3 credits)

- Managerial Accounting Straighterline course* (3 credits)

- Introductory Business Law CLEP (3 credits)

- Information Systems & Computer Applications CLEP (3 credits)

- Principles of Management CLEP (3 credits)

- Principles of Marketing CLEP (3 credits)

- Principles of Finance DSST (3 credits)

- Operations Management TECEP (3 credits)

- Organizational Behavior ECE (3 credits)

- Business Ethics & Society DSST (3 credits)

- Business Policy Excelsior Online Course (3 credits)*

Advanced-Level Business Credit (12 credits)
- Business Law 2 DSST (3 credits)

- Money & Banking DSST (3 credits)

- Management Information Systems DSST (3 credits)

- Human Resource Management ECE (3 credits)

Additional Credit Component
- Personal Finance DSST (3 credits)

- Intro to World Religions DSST (3 credits)

- Technical Writing DSST (3 credits)

- Principles of Public Speaking DSST (3 credits)

- Physical Geography DSST (3 credits)

- Information Literacy Excelsior Online Course (1 credit)*

TOTAL CREDITS TO BE EARNED: 121

NOTE: If you're fluent in French, German or Spanish, the CLEP exams in these subjects are worth 12 credits. This could be your entire Additional Credit component (or a 12 credit chunk of your Arts & Sciences component.) Remember to reference the DIY Degree "Exam List" spreadsheet to intelligently and strategically pick which exams you take. Pay special attention to the "exam strategy" points on rapid credit accumulation.

The stars above indicate credits for which there are, sadly, no exams. There used to be a CLEP exam that covered Managerial Accounting, but no longer. As for Business Policy, there actually is a TECEP exam for it, but Excelsior insists that all students take at least that one class through them. Information Literacy is a 1 credit online course that all Excelsior students are required to complete regardless of degree choice. Don't worry: it's just a refresher on how to do research in libraries and on the web. I completed this "course" in 1 hour.

Again: other schools may require you to take a small number of courses in addition to your exams. Don't let this distract you from the bigger picture. Online courses at these schools are still a fraction of what you would pay even at a local community college, and you will still be earning the vast majority of your degree with inexpensive exams or Portfolio Learning Assessment.

In the next chapter, I've provided a blank DIY Degree gameplan that you can fill out and keep nearby for easy progress tracking.

To watch over my shoulder as I build a fully fleshed-out degree plan, visit:
www.DoItYourselfDegree.com/watch-learn

Chapter 10: Filling Out Your DIY Degree Gameplan

Below, I've included a blank DIY Degree Gameplan template for you to fill out.

For minimum confusion, keep the following in front of you while filling this out:

- Excelsior's "Degree Overview" for the degree you're pursuing (or the equivalent document from any other school you chose)
- The sample DIY Degree Gameplan from the last chapter
- The chapter on "Connecting All Requirements & Electives to Exams" (so you can use the exam strategies to your benefit)

My DIY Degree Gameplan

Arts & Sciences Component

- <u>Introductory Psychology CLEP</u> exam at <u>10AM</u> on <u>November 10</u> at <u>Patrick Henry University</u>
- _____ exam at ____ on _____ at _____
- _____ exam at ____ on _____ at _____
- _____ exam at ____ on _____ at _____
- _____ exam at ____ on _____ at _____

- _____ exam at _____ on _____ at _____

- _____ exam at _____ on _____ at _____

- _____ exam at _____ on _____ at _____

- _____ exam at _____ on _____ at _____

- _____ exam at _____ on _____ at _____

- _____ exam at _____ on _____ at _____

- _____ exam at _____ on _____ at _____

- _____ exam at _____ on _____ at _____

- _____ exam at _____ on _____ at _____

- _____ exam at _____ on _____ at _____

- _____ exam at _____ on _____ at _____

-

Core Classes Component

- _____ exam at _____ on _____ at _____

- _____ exam at _____ on _____ at _____

- _____ exam at ____ on _____ at
  _____
- _____ exam at ____ on _____ at
  _____
- _____ exam at ____ on _____ at
  _____
- _____ exam at ____ on _____ at
  _____
- _____ exam at ____ on _____ at
  _____
- _____ exam at ____ on _____ at
  _____
- _____ exam at ____ on _____ at
  _____
- _____ exam at ____ on _____ at
  _____
- _____ exam at ____ on _____ at
  _____

Advanced-Level Credit

- _____ exam at ____ on _____ at
  _____
- _____ exam at ____ on _____ at
  _____
- _____ exam at ____ on _____ at
  _____
- _____ exam at ____ on _____ at
  _____

Additional Credit Component

- _____ exam at _____ on _____ at
  _____

- _____ exam at _____ on _____ at
  _____

- _____ exam at _____ on _____ at
  _____

- _____ exam at _____ on _____ at
  _____

- _____ exam at _____ on _____ at
  _____

- _____ exam at _____ on _____ at
  _____

The beauty of this Gameplan is that you don't need to fill everything out at once. If you know which exams you want to take (but not when you're going to take them, or which testing centers you'll use) you can just write in the name of the exams and fill in the rest later.

In any case, all the key information will always be in one centralized place. This will cut down on confusion and keep you motivated. Also, you may not need every space provided in this Gameplan. If you take exams worth 6 or 12 credits, for example, there will surely be a few blank spaces. Nothing wrong with that - in fact, that would be ideal!

Also keep in mind what I said about using psychology against yourself. Schedule five or six exams at a time so that you're always studying and progressing to the next test.

Now it's time to show this Gameplan to Excelsior's academic advisors. These are the people who can tell you, with certainty, whether it will work. They can also make corrections, so that you can change your DIY Degree Gameplan if necessary.

The next chapter includes exactly what to say to the advisors, including word-for-word emails you can use with minimal changes.

Chapter 11: Getting Your DIY Degree Gameplan Approved

One of the most fascinating things I've learned in recent years is the psychology of passive barriers.

Basically, passive barriers are things that don't exist, and therefore, make your life harder. For example: you know that enrolling in your employer's 401(k) program is a smart decision, but you don't know HOW to do it. Which number do you call? What forms do you fill out? How much should you set aside from each week's check? What about the tax implications?

"Those are such small problems", you might say. Surely, no one who's serious about saving for retirement would let these obstacles stop them. You'd think so...but you'd be wrong. In one company, when it was up to employees to opt **in** to the plan, only 40% of them did. But when the company changed its policy so that you were automatically enrolled and had to opt OUT, nearly 100% of employees participated.

What changed? The barrier was removed. In fact, the barrier was reversed. It was easier for people to stay in the 401(k) plan they already belonged to than to figure out how to leave.

Here are a few more examples from Ramit Sethi's amazing article, "The Psychology of Passive Barriers"

Barriers in sex

Psychologists have been studying college students for decades to understand how to reduce unprotected sex. Among the most interesting findings, they pointed out that it would be rational for women to carry condoms with them, since the sexual experiences they had were often unplanned and these women can control the use of contraceptives.

Except for one thing: When they asked college women why they didn't carry condoms with them, one young woman typified the responses: "I couldn't do that...I'd seem slutty." As a result, she and others often ended up having unprotected sex because of the lack of a condom. Yes, technically they should carry condoms, just as both partners should stop, calmly go to the corner liquor store, and get protection. But many times, they don't.

In this case, the condom was the passive barrier: Because they didn't have it nearby and conveniently available, they violated their own rule to have safe sex.

Barriers in e-mail

I get emails like this all the time:

"Hey Ramit, what do you think of that article I sent last week? Any suggested changes?"

My reaction? "Ugh, what is he talking about? Oh yeah, that article on savings accounts...I have to dig that up and reply to him. Where is that? I'll search for it later. Marks email as unread"

Note: You can yell at me for not just taking the 30 seconds to find his email right then, but that's exactly the point: By not including the article in this follow up email, he triggered a passive barrier of me needing to think about what he was talking about, search for it, and then decide what to reply to. The lack of the attached article is the passive barrier, and our most common response to barriers is to do nothing.

Barriers on your desk

A friend of mine lost over $3,000 because he didn't cash a check from his workplace, which went bankrupt a few months later. When I asked him why he didn't cash the check immediately, he looked at me and said, "I didn't have an envelope handy." What other things do you delay because it's not convenient?

Barriers to exercise

I think back to when I've failed to hit my workout goals, and it's often the simplest of reasons. One of the most obvious barriers was my workout clothes. I had one pair of running pants, and after each workout, I would throw it in my laundry basket. When I woke up the next morning, the first thing I would think is: "Oh god, I have to get up, claw through my dirty clothes, and wear those sweaty pants again."

Once I identified this, I bought a second pair of workout clothes and left them by my door each day. When I woke up, I knew I could walk out of my room, find the fully prepared workout bag and clothes, and get going.

Passive barriers in the DIY Degree approach

Obstacles like these seem trivial, but when they accumulate, they can be VERY overwhelming. As a result, we find it easier to do nothing than to confront these pesky barriers. And as I went about finishing my degree the DIY way, I saw that there were a TON of passive barriers hidden like landmines throughout the process.

In this chapter, we're going to confront one of the biggest ones: getting your DIY Degree Gameplan approved.

This is where a lot of people get stuck. They love the *theory* of earning their degree independently. They know they're capable of passing their exams. But how do they know that their Gameplan will actually work? Who do they ask? What do they say? What if their plan IS wrong?

Luckily for you, I've anticipated these barriers and taken them out of your way. Here's exactly what to do once you've created your DIY Degree Gameplan.

Simply send this email to your academic advisor

On the next page, I've included an entire, word-for-word email that you can send directly to your academic advisor. All you'll need to change are the exams you plan on taking. The rest of the email is designed to make the advisor confirm to you that your plan will work - or, if not, tell you specifically how to fix it.

There are actually two emails I want to share with you. The first, below, is for people who are earning their entire degree the DIY way. Use this email if you have no prior college credit and are starting from square one:

> Hi,
>
> My name is _____. I was recently admitted to Excelsior's School of Business & Technology. My student ID number is _____. I am pursuing a bachelor's degree in General Business (OR OTHER DEGREE.) I have not yet earned any college credit. Instead, I am aiming to complete my entire degree using the credit-by-examination method.
>
> My academic plan has arrived and I know which credits I need to earn.
>
> What I'd like to do below is share my personal gameplan for earning them. And, hopefully, get approval from you that my plan will actually work.
>
> Below is a complete list of which exams I plan to take, which credit requirements they will satisfy, and how many credits each one is worth.
>
> ### Arts & Sciences Component (60 credits)
> - College Composition Modular CLEP (3 credits)
> - American Government CLEP (3 credits)
> - Introductory Psychology CLEP (3 credits)
> - Introductory Sociology CLEP (3 credits)
> - Principles of Microeconomics CLEP (3 credits)
> - Principles of Macroeconomics CLEP (3 credits)
> - Social Sciences & History CLEP (6 credits)
> - History of United States 1 CLEP (3 credits)

- Principles of Statistics ALEKS course (3 credits)
- Pre-calculus ALEKS course (3 credits)
- Ethics in America CLEP (3 credits)
- History of United States 2 CLEP (3 credits)
- Western Civilization 1 CLEP (3 credits)
- Western Civilization 2 CLEP (3 credits)
- Biology CLEP (6 credits)
- Humanities CLEP (6 credits)
- Human Growth & Development CLEP (3 credits)

Business Component (45 credits)
- Financial Accounting CLEP (3 credits)
- Managerial Accounting Straighterline course* (3 credits)
- Introductory Business Law CLEP (3 credits)
- Information Systems & Computer Applications CLEP (3 credits)
- Principles of Management CLEP (3 credits)
- Principles of Marketing CLEP (3 credits)
- Principles of Finance DSST (3 credits)
- Operations Management TECEP (3 credits)
- Organizational Behavior ECE (3 credits)
- Business Ethics & Society DSST (3 credits)
- Business Policy Excelsior Online Course (3 credits)*

Advanced-Level Business Credit (12 credits)
- Business Law 2 DSST (3 credits)
- Money & Banking DSST (3 credits)
- Management Information Systems DSST (3 credits)
- Human Resource Management ECE (3 credits)

Additional Credit Component

- Personal Finance DSST (3 credits)
- Intro to World Religions DSST (3 credits)
- Technical Writing DSST (3 credits)
- Principles of Public Speaking DSST (3 credits)
- Physical Geography DSST (3 credits)
- Information Literacy Excelsior Online Course (1 credit)*

TOTAL CREDITS TO BE EARNED: 121

Can you confirm that this plan will, in fact, lead to my bachelor's degree in General Business? Or, if I've made any mistakes, please point them out and suggest alternative exams that would work?

I appreciate your fastest response. Thanks so much for helping me!

Best,

- YOURNAME

Now, the second email, below, is for people WITH college credits, who want to FINISH their degree the DIY way. Since this is what I did, I'm actually going to paste in the exact email that I used, so you'll know how to approach this. Obviously, insert your own name, student number, degree program, etc. I'm just showing the word-for-word email so you can see what the finished product looks like:

Hi,

My name is Jay Cross. I was recently admitted to Excelsior's School of Business & Technology. Student ID number is [REDACTED]. I am pursuing a bachelor's degree in General Business. My academic plan has arrived and I know which credits I need to earn.

What I'd like to do below is share my personal game plan for obtaining those credits. And (hopefully) get the green light from you that it will work.

Excelsior recognizes that I have earned 86 credits to date. As I understand it, the minimum required to graduate with my degree is 120 credits.

My remaining required credits are: Information Literacy, Introduction To United States Business Law, Principles of Marketing, Financial Management, Product/Operations Management, Business Policy, Organizational Behavior, Statistics, and Math (pre-calc or above.)

I intend to:

- Take **CLEP** exams for Marketing and Business Law
- Take the **DSST** exam for Principles of Finance
- Take the **Excelsior** exam for Organizational Behavior
- Take **ALEKS** online courses for Statistics and Pre-Calculus
- Take **TECEP** exam for Operations Management
- Take **Excelsior online courses** (beginning in March) for Information Literacy and Business Strategy (which, as I understand, is equal to BUS*495)

[NOTE TO READERS: these were the courses I, myself, still needed at the time. Yours will differ. That's okay - just open up the DIY Degree Exam List in your Member's Area and find exams that will satisfy YOUR requirements. Then list them out here the way that I did.]

This should generate 25 credits, which, when added to my current 86, gives me 111. To earn the remaining 9 credits needed to graduate, I wish to take **Excelsior** exams for the following:

○ Social Psychology
○ Bioethics: Philosophical Issues

This should bring me to 117 credits. For my last 3 credits, I would like to take the **DSST** exam for Technical Writing. Unless I'm missing something, this should complete my degree and allow me to graduate in late 2011/early 2012.

I realize this is a rather ambitious plan. However, I have taken on huge course loads before and am not at all intimidated by the challenge. In fact, I actually cannot wait to get started! My Marketing CLEP is scheduled for next week.

Can you please confirm that this course of action will lead to my degree, or, if not, help me correct course?

Thanks so much!

- Jay

Notice several things about these emails:

First, I eliminated the barrier of them having to look up my student number. I also made sure to tell them that I already saw my academic plan (so they couldn't say "go look at your academic plan" and ignore the rest of my email.) Next, I TOLD THEM what my remaining credits were, so they wouldn't have to figure it out themselves.

Then, I listed my Gameplan - not just which credits I still needed, but the EXACT EXAMS I would take to earn them. I told the entire story, explaining why I choose those exams and what I believed the outcome of passing them would be.

Finally (and this is crucial) I closed by asking them to EITHER confirm that my plan would work OR help me correct course. This was no accident. Using my training as a copywriter (and my knowledge of passive barriers) I consciously designed this email to get the answers I needed. That includes eliminating every reason for not answering helpfully.

Which they did. The same day, I received the following response, containing some very important corrections:

> Hello Jay,
>
> Your plan looks pretty good. However once you complete the specific required courses, you need the 12 Advanced level Business Electives. The Excelsior College Organizational Behavior exam will meet both the requirement and three credits of Advanced level Business. Therefore you need three more courses or exams in Business electives at the advanced

level. We also offer exams in Labor Relations and Human Resource Management. DANTES has Money & Banking, Business Law II, and Management Information Systems which are advanced level Business.

When you finish the exams/courses in your plan you will have a total of 111
credits. Then the three advanced level Business elective exams or courses
will make up the needed 9 credits for total of 120.

Respectfully,
[REDACTED]
Senior Academic Advisor

School of Business and Technology

BAM! In less than two hours, a simple email crushed all my doubts and gave me huge motivation to get started...because I KNEW MY PLAN WOULD WORK.

Now it's time for all your preparation and planning to start paying off. The next chapter focuses on actually executing your newly approved DIY Degree Gameplan.

Chapter 12: Executing Your DIY Degree Gameplan

The time for talk is over.

You've enrolled at Excelsior (or another distance-learning school), chosen a degree program, mapped out a DIY Degree Gameplan and confirmed that it will work. Now it's time for the hardest (and most important) phase of any goal: the "actually doin' it" phase.

With the DIY Degree, "actually doin' it" means studying for and taking the exams in your Gameplan. Studying is a huge part this, so I want to share some study tips with you that have been helpful to me over the years.

How to study for maximum exam performance

We often hear that some people are naturally "test-takers" while others are not. I think that's BS. As far as I can see, the difference between so-called "test-takers" and everyone else is that test-takers have better study habits. Here are some of them:

- **Study concepts, not minutiae.** Most people who test poorly are simply studying the wrong things. They erroneously believe that they need to memorize *every* fact, *every* date, *every* name, acronym or abbreviation in order to pass. And invariably, they end up getting bogged down in little stuff, rather than paying attention to the broad, overarching, key concepts the professor really wants you to learn. Example: if you're studying for the Psychology CLEP, pay way less attention to the fact that Ivan Pavlov discovered classical conditioning, and way more attention to what classical conditioning IS. At most, there'll be one question about Pavlov, but there'll be several scenario questions about classical conditioning itself. Ditto for Human Resource Management: don't sweat WHEN the Labor Relations Board came into existence...focus on what it was established to do.

- **Take notes in your own words instead of copying.** Another thing I always notice poor test-takers doing is copying their notes straight out textbooks. The problem with this approach is that you aren't really absorbing the material. You're just mimicking what someone else wrote and patting yourself on the back for "taking notes." Good test-takers, on the other hand, take notes more deliberately. Rather than simply copying the author's description of a concept, they'll take a minute, think about it, and write it in their own words. The act of putting something into your own words forces you to UNDERSTAND what you're studying instead of merely letting it wash over you.

EXAMPLE: SOCIAL LOAFING

A poor test-taker, when taking notes on this concept, would write: "Social loafing is the phenomenon of people exerting less effort to achieve a goal when they work in a group than when they work alone." In other words, the basic, terse, verbatim textbook definition.

A good test-taker, when taking notes on the same concept, would write something like: "Social loafing is when everyone in a group assumes that someone else is taking care of important tasks and that they, therefore, can slack off. An example would be group work at college. One person usually takes on a huge share of the work while the others lag behind, knowing they'll benefit from that person's effort."

- **Study in small, spaced-out sessions rather than all at once.** We're told not to cram so often that it sounds like worthless advice. However, it's important to realize that there is actual brain science behind this. Our minds are much better at absorbing information in manageable increments than cramming everything in one shot. That's why, for most people, it's way better to study for an hour a night over 2 weeks than for 8 hours the night before an exam.

- **Study before sleeping.** Scientists are beginning to find that we retain what we learn just before sleeping more effectively than what we learn during the day.

"A Nova: Science Now documentary in 2007 rallied the evidence for learning improvement during sleep. One interesting experiment involved microelectrodes implanted into the brains of rats. Each microelectrode could record from a dozen nerve cells, and the tips of the electrodes were in regions of the rat's brain that processed movements during a run through a maze.

As the rat successfully navigated the maze, the neurons fired in a distinctive pattern. Later, as the rats slept, the researchers observed those same neurons firing in the same distinctive pattern. **This suggested that the rats were reliving the successful run through the maze, in their dreams.** Other researchers showed that memory for experimental tasks improved for all sorts of animals, even fruit flies, if the animals were allowed to sleep or rest during the night instead of being kept up and active." (Nova Science Now, July 14, 2007)

If possible, try to squeeze in a study session or two before bed: especially when it comes to the really challenging parts of a subject.

Study resources

One of the most common questions people ask about the DIY Degree approach is "how do I study?" Thanks to the DIY Degree Exam Master List I created for you, you'll know what's ON the exams. Just download the study guide or fact sheet for a full topic breakdown. As for actually studying those topics, I recommend the following.

There are a few resources that I used to study for my exams

The first is an excellent (and FREE) website called **http://www.free-clep-prep.com/**. This website contains a bevy of study guides and recommendations for almost every exam there is. Each exam page lists a complete breakdown of topics, how much they count for, and links to websites where you can study them.

Just select which exam you're studying for and you'll get complete access to all of these materials. Free-Clep-Prep.com also lists outside resources to help you study for each exam (like inexpensive prep books you can order from Amazon.)

The other website I used extensively is **www.instantcert.com**. This is a paid service (about $15 per month) but it is unquestionably worth it. What you get here is a complete set of flashcards for every single exam. These flashcards contain VERBATIM what you'll see on each test.

InstantCert
A C A D E M Y

Customize your Operations Management TECEP Question Set

Database currently contains 297 questions.
Randomize the order of the questions

Select which topics you would like covered:
Operations Management TECEP Sections
- Systems Management [60 Questions]
- Systems Design [59 Questions]
- Systems Planning, Analysis, and Control Part 1 [39 Questions]
- Systems Planning, Analysis, and Control Part 2 [29 Questions]
- Systems Planning, Analysis, and Control Part 3 [56 Questions]
- Systems Planning, Analysis, and Control Part 4 [54 Questions]

InstantCert has flashcard sets like this for nearly every exam in the DIY Degree Master Exam List spreadsheet.

Study these flashcards in the weeks leading up to an exam. Take notes. Write out the material in your own words, so you actually understand it (as opposed to just memorizing.) Note also that these study materials, while outstanding, are not exhaustive. The exams you'll be taking are intended to cover a semester's worth of knowledge in that subject. So it IS possible to see a question or two on an exam that wasn't covered in Instantcert.

Now, having said all that, here's an important caveat...
Services like InstantCert are great for brushing on subjects you have some level of familiarity with. But what about passing subjects you literally know nothing about? In those cases, flashcards are unlikely to instill the deep understanding needed to pass a challenging exam for credit.

For these subjects, you will want to buy inexpensive used textbooks to thoroughly study the concepts you will encounter on your exams.

Now, I know what you're thinking, because new DIY Degree students email this question to me constantly...

"Wait! Are you saying I need to read textbooks cover to cover before I can pass these tests? I'd never have time!"

No. I'm NOT saying that. Far from it! In fact, every subject you need to pass falls into one of four subject clusters:

- Informational Subjects (like biology, history, law, management, psychology, etc.)
- Interpretive Subjects (like art history, English, philosophy, literature, etc.)
- Problem-Solving Subjects (like accounting, chemistry, math, finance, etc.)
- Creative Subjects (like creative writing, foreign language, music, theater, etc.)

The key to fast and effective studying is to use the correct study techniques for the cluster you find yourself in at the moment.

Your biggest challenge: staying motivated for the long haul

I'm not going to lie to you. The DIY Degree approach is the most convenient and pain-free way to earn an associate's or bachelor's degree that I know of. But although it's the *easiest* way, that does not mean it will be "easy."

I didn't just pick the name "Do-It-Yourself Degree" because it was catchy and memorable. It's also 100% accurate. You **will** be doing this yourself - all of it! I can give you the weapons for the battle, but I can't carry you to the front lines. That's where motivation comes in.

Studying for exams can be frustrating. Making time to read and take notes is annoying. On any given day, there will be a dozen things you'd rather immerse yourself in than psychology or western civilization or statistics. The temptation to procrastinate will always be there, begging you to give in. It certainly was for me.

That's why I've encouraged you to use psychology and systems against yourself, by scheduling lots of exams at a time, scheduling them close together and taking easier ones first. Without these powerful environmental forces propelling you forward, human nature will slow you down.

It's also why I included the DIY Degree Gameplan template with this book. That is intended for you to post in a place where you always see it, where it will serve as a constant reminder of where you started, where you are now, and where you're going.

I know you can do this. It won't always be easy, and it won't always be fun, but in the end, you will succeed - and it will be worth the struggle.

Feel free to email me (**jay@doityourselfdegree.com**) along the way. I'd love to hear how your journey toward a DIY Degree is going. And if there's anything I haven't covered for you, just ask!

Chapter 13: Closing Thoughts
Succeeding AFTER Earning Your
DIY Degree

I heard something while writing the DIY Degree that was so true. It's a quote from Charlie Hoen about the value of college:

> "You need to understand that college degrees are not given to unique snowflake children."

So many of us believe that "a degree", by its very existence, will make us irresistible to employers. But really, as Charlie indicates, that isn't true. A degree, though certainly valuable, is not the END of your quest to succeed. It's just the beginning.

The truth is, degrees are becoming commoditized. Twenty years ago, having your bachelor's was impressive enough to set you apart from the crowd. Today, it's a baseline necessity. Everyone has one - or, at least, most do.

To stand out in today's job marketplace, you need to do more than just have a degree on your resume. You need to go about your career in a totally different way than most people do. In this closing chapter, I'd like to offer you some suggestions on doing this, followed by some books, blogs, and articles that have helped me in my quest to succeed.

- **Consider self-employment.** Too many of us are trapped in the idea that we HAVE to work for someone else. It's not true. Self-employment is a lot more realistic than you might think. Fundamentally, you just need to provide some good or service to people who want it and do so at a profit. You can be a writer, a graphic designer, a housekeeper - literally anything, so long as people are willing to pay you for it. Find people who want what you can offer and sell yourself to them. I'm over-simplifying, but this is really what it boils down to. If you don't like your job, don't find a new one: create your own.

- **Look for the RIGHT job, not just "a job."** How many times have you heard someone complaining about how "no one" will hire them? How they just want "a job, any job?" Look: sometimes, you have to do what you have to do. Maybe that means taking a job you aren't excited about for a few months to keep the lights on. Long-term, though, you should be thinking about the RIGHT job, not just any random job you can get. After all, who is likely to be more successful: someone with no clear objectives, taking the "shotgun at the wall" approach of applying to every classified ad...or someone who knows exactly which job he wants and pursues it with focus and determination?

- **Don't just list your degree, position it!** Some might say the DIY Degree puts you at a disadvantage. Colleges like Excelsior and Thomas Edison (though certainly legitimate) aren't the biggest-name schools out there. Yet if you're strategic, you can actually use this to your advantage. Turn your DIY Degree into a strength during job interviews by playing up the way you got it. Talk about how it was a completely independent and self-managed approach. Talk about how you not only designed your entire degree plan yourself, but also scheduled, studied for, and passed anywhere from 25-40 challenging exams in under a year. This shows an incredible amount of self-discipline and time management skill. Most people would NEVER do what you did.

Books, blogs, and articles that have helped me succeed

Here are just a handful of my favorite success resources. I hope you get as much value out of them as I did!

Succeeding, by John T. Reed

Most success books encourage you to pursue whatever arbitrary goals you already happen to have. Make millions of dollars, become famous, travel the world - whatever your heart desires. "Succeeding" takes a more nuanced approach, helping you identify the RIGHT goals and increase your chances of achieving them. Reed is a blunt writer, and you won't always agree with his views, but that's okay. As best-selling "E-Myth" author Michael Gerber once said, "the only time someone's telling you the truth is when it's pissing you off."

Learn more at: http://www.johntreed.com/succeeding.html

I Will Teach You To Be Rich, by Ramit Sethi

The typical personal finance book contains ancient, condescending advice that nobody follows. Make a budget. Never eat at restaurants. Stop buying lattes. It always about saying no to yourself - and that's why it never works. "I Will Teach You To Be Rich" is different. Rather than telling us to endlessly sacrifice, IWT explains how to use systems and psychology to buy what you want without feeling guilty about it. "Spend lavishly on things you love, while cutting costs mercilessly on things you don't" is the key message. Ramit is as sharp as they come, and his *New York Times* best-seller will change your outlook on more than just money.

Learn more at: http://www.iwillteachyoutoberich.com

How To Do What You Love, by Paul Graham

"Do what you love" is repeated so often that it's almost a cliche. But we rarely talk about HOW to do what you love, or what it actually requires in practice. This essay, written by Y Combinator's Paul Graham, is exclusively about that. My favorite passage:

> "You have to like what you do enough that the concept of "spare time" seems mistaken. Which is not to say you have to spend all your time working. You can only work so much before you get tired and start to screw up. Then you want to do something else—even something mindless. But you don't regard this time as the prize and the time you spend working as the pain you endure to earn it."

This is one of my favorite essays of all time. Highly recommended.

Learn more at: http://www.paulgraham.com/love.html

Create More, Consume Less, by ArtOfManliness.com

An incredibly thought-provoking essay on why it's more satisfying to create than consume. A favorite passage:

"Men have an inherent desire to be creators, to change the landscape, to turn wood into furniture, to transform a blank canvas into a work of art-to alter the world and leave a legacy. It's the denial of this aspect of manliness that is perhaps most plaguing modern men. Young men are taught to think of life past 30 as a certain death, a time when they have to stop being selfish and live for others. The paradox that's never talked about is that consuming is the real dead end when it comes to happiness. Your mind gets caught in an fruitless cycle-new experiences initially give you intense pleasure, but the more you consume of it, the more saturated your pleasure sensors become until you have to ratchet up the intensity and quantity of the experience to get the same "high" you used to. And the cycle endlessly continues.

But when you create instead of consume, your capacity for pleasure increases, as opposed to your need for it. Being a creator gives you a far more lasting and deeply satisfying happiness than consuming ever will."

Learn more at: http://artofmanliness.com/2010/04/06/modern-maturity-create-more-consume-less/

Ultimately, I hope that you go on to not just earn your degree, but create a life that you love. I
also hope that you will tell me how your quest goes. What your struggles were, improvements to the DIY Degree process that you discovered, or even just an update on what you're up to.

Email me anytime at **jay@doityourselfdegree.com**.

If you need some help, don't forget: you can watch over my shoulder as I build a fully fleshed-out degree plan by visiting: **www.DoItYourselfDegree.com/watch-learn**

Or, if you would like us to personally build a DIY Degree custom graduation roadmap FOR YOU, visit:
www.DoItYourselfDegree.com/done-for-you

Good luck!

To your success,

- Jay

Made in the USA
San Bernardino, CA
30 December 2016